Theory Paper Grade 3   2016   A
Model Answers

1 (10)

2 *There are many ways of completing this question. The specimen completion below would receive full marks.* (10)

3 (10)

(a)

(b)

4   F sharp   D/ D natural   E flat   (10)
      A / A natural   C sharp   D flat

5   F♯ minor   G major   C minor   (10)

      E♭ major   E minor

3

6 (10)

7   perfect   perfect   major   (10)
      5th   octave / 8ve / 8th   7th

                  minor   major
                  6th   2nd

8   (a)   fairly quick / quite quick / quick, but not as quick as allegro   (10)
              simple / plain
              accent / forced / accented
              play the notes smoothly / slur
              getting louder / gradually getting louder

        (b)   (10)
              (i)   7th
              (ii)   D major
              (iii) true
              (iv)   compound
                     duple
              (v)   six

        (c)   (10)

Theory Paper Grade 3   2016   B
Model Answers

1   (10)

2 *There are many ways of completing this question. The specimen completion below would receive full marks.* (10)

3 (10)

4 (10)

5 (10)

6 (10)

7 (10)

(a)

(b) simple
quadruple

5

8 (a) slow / stately (10)
  expressive / expressively / with expression
  the number of beats in a bar / two beats in a bar
  quiet / soft
  getting louder / gradually getting louder

  (b) (10)
    (i) G
    (ii) B♭ major
    (iii) demisemiquaver / 32nd note
    (iv) 4th
    (v) false

  (c) (10)

or 𝄵

Theory Paper Grade 3   2016   C
Model Answers

1 (10)

2 *There are many ways of completing this question. The specimen completion below would receive full marks.* (10)

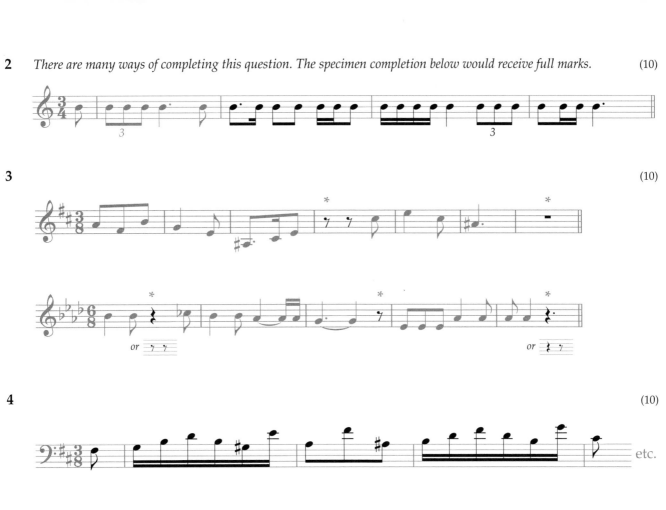

3 (10)

4 (10)

5 (10)

6 (10)

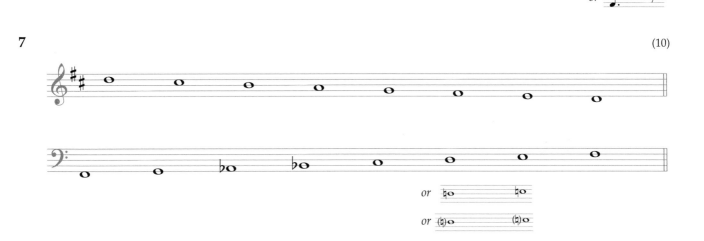

7 (10)

8 (a)   (10)

      (i)   graceful / gracefully / with grace
              much / very
              simple / plain
              quiet / soft

      (ii)   simple
             triple

(b)   (10)

      (i)   six
      (ii)   four
      (iii)   *There are two possible answers to this question. Either circle shown would receive full marks.*

      (iv)   E
      (v)   true

(c)   (10)

Theory Paper Grade 3   2016   S
Model Answers

1   (10)

2   *There are many ways of completing this question. The specimen completion below would receive full marks.*   (10)

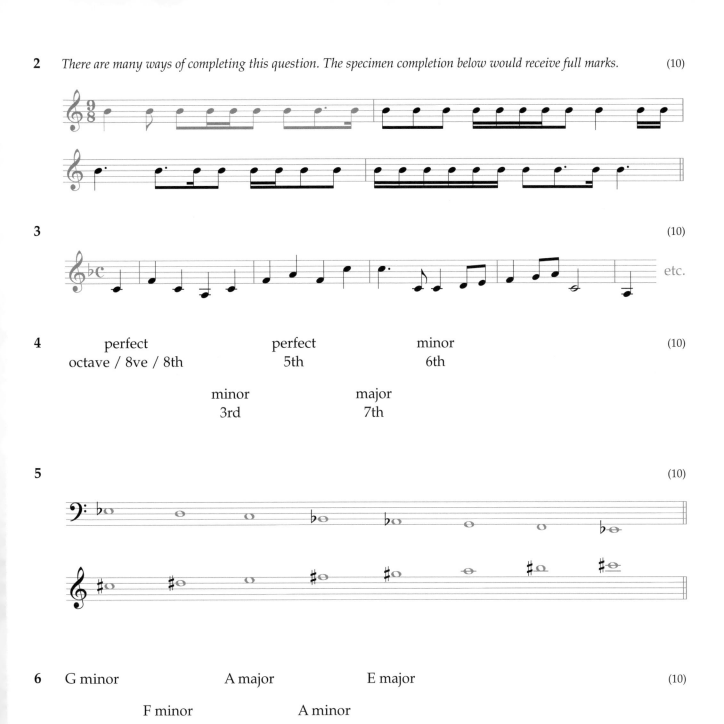

3   (10)

etc.

4   (10)

perfect
octave / 8ve / 8th

perfect
5th

minor
6th

minor
3rd

major
7th

5   (10)

6   G minor   A major   E major   (10)

F minor   A minor

7   (10)

(a)

(b)   six

8 (a) fast / quick / cheerful / lively   (10)
   not so much
   very loud
   accent / forced / accented
   play the notes detached / jumpy / staccato

(b)   (10)

   (i)

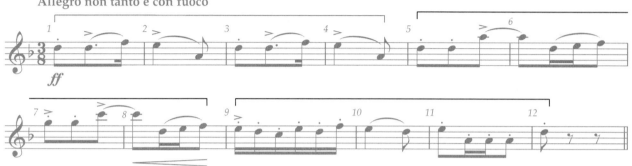

   (ii) simple
        triple
   (iii) two
   (iv) Similarity   rhythm / slur / first note tied from previous bar
        Difference   pitch of first note / hairpin
   (v) C

(c)   (10)

Music Theory Past Papers 2016 Model Answers

Model answers for four past papers from ABRSM's 2016 Theory exams for Grade 3

Key features:

- a list of correct answers where appropriate
- a selection of likely options where the answer can be expressed in a variety of ways
- a single exemplar where a composition-style answer is required

Support material for ABRSM Music Theory exams

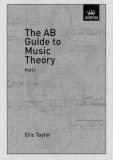

Supporting the teaching and learning of music in partnership with the Royal Schools of Music

Royal Academy of Music | Royal College of Music
Royal Northern College of Music | Royal Conservatoire of Scotland

www.abrsm.org **f** facebook.com/abrsm
𝕏 @abrsm ▶ ABRSM YouTube

ISBN 978-1-84849-815-0

9 781848 498150